THE KING OF THINGS
AND THE
CRANBERRY CLOWN

THE KING OF THINGS AND THE CRANBERRY CLOWN

John Callahan

WILLIAM MORROW AND COMPANY, INC.

NEW YORK

It is the policy of William Morrow and Company, Inc., and its imprints and affiliates,
recognizing the importance of preserving what has been written, to print the books
we publish on acid-free paper, and we exert our best efforts to that end.

LIBRARY OF CONGRESS CATALOGING-IN-PUBLICATION DATA

Callahan, John.
The king of things and the cranberry clown / by John Callahan.
p.   cm.
ISBN 0-688-13975-2
1. Kings and rulers—Poetry.   2. Clowns—Poetry.   I. Title.
PS3553.A42165K56   1995
811′.54—dc20   94-12781
CIP

Printed in the United States of America

First Edition

1   2   3   4   5   6   7   8   9   10

For bobby
(Dylan)

THE KING OF THINGS
AND THE
CRANBERRY CLOWN

The King of Things
was busy one day,
making sure things
were going his way.

The piggies were dancing
just the way that he loved,
when he pulled on his strings
or gave them a shove.

9

His strings were hooked up
to the ducks by their bills,
and he controlled all the quacking
on Cranberry Hill.

He controlled all the gators
and the sharks in the pond,
and everything else
they were chomping upon.

And the moon and the stars
were his just to spin,
and he played them his way
like a violin.

He controlled all the faces,
the laughs and the frowns,
he controlled all the colors,
the lights and the sounds.

He controlled the whole world
with the strings that he had,
he controlled everything,
for good or for bad.

When the King of Things
was sleepy, he'd sleep,
and the strings in his dreams
pulled the strings on the sheep.

And when he awoke,
he wanted his way,
and he pulled on a string
for treats on a tray.

Now, the King's only friend
was a quarrelsome crow,
who teased him on Tuesdays
about things he should know.

"Such a powerful King!"
said the crow as she joked.
"But where would he be
if his strings ever broke?"

"But my strings never break!"
said the King with great pride.
But the thought of them breaking
made him shudder inside.

And it made him so nervous
it tied him in knots,
and after a while
he controlled his own thoughts.

And so it was
as the years passed the rings,
the world was in chains
to the King of Things.

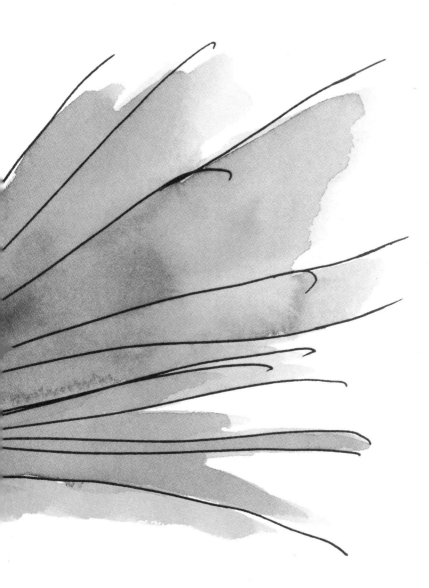

23

One day the quarrelsome crow
came to visit,
and the King scratched his head
and demanded, "What is it?"

"The people are angry!
And the piggies are, too!
And the duckies and the gators
and the kangaroos!"

"And the moon and the stars
and the sun up above,
and everything else
you push and you shove!"

"What do you know
of these things!" cried the King.
"These matters of power,
control, and of string!"

"Of pushing and pulling
all day and all night,
so that everything everywhere
works out just right."

"There's nothing I know,
and there's nothing I'll say!
But there's someone who does,
and you'll meet him someday!"

"Who's that?" said the King,
with his face in a frown.
"His name," said the crow,
"is the Cranberry Clown!"

29

One day a stranger
appeared on the hill,
and the King scratched his head
by the windowsill.

"Who's that?" said he,
to the quarrelsome crow.
"It's the Cranberry Clown!
I thought you would know!"

He sat all alone
at the top of the knoll,
and he was tangled in string
from his neck to his soles.

The string was so tight
the clown couldn't budge.
Not a shoulder to shirk,
nor an elbow to nudge.

He moved not a finger,
a leg nor a toe,
and he'd given up trying
a long time ago.

"What does he do?"
said the King, with a sniff.
"He sits all alone,
and he falls off a cliff."

"What's that?" said the King.
"What did you say?"
"It's true," said the crow,
"he does it all day!"

"He closes his eyes,
and he tips his chair,
and he holds his breath,
and he falls somewhere."

The years passed again,
and the King only worsened,
as he tightened his grip
on each thing and each person.

"You'll all do my will!"
he cried from the hill.
But the more he insisted,
the more they resisted.

The King grew angry,
and he started to pout,
when the voice of the quarrelsome
crow rang out.

41

Everyone watched her
as she soared high above.
The King was shaking,
and he dropped his silk glove.

"Everyone here
and everything, too,
is a King in this world,
just like you."

"We all have our wishes,
and we all want our way,
but the game doesn't work
when someone won't play!"

"You've had many chances,
and you've scoffed at each one,
now it's the end of your mischief,
it's the end of your fun!"

45

"Now, everyone listen,
the whole world over!
Whether high in the sky,
or deep in the clover!"

"When I count to two,
pull away at your strings,
and break your connection
to the King of Things!"

The King held hard
to the strings in his hand,
but the force that he felt
was more than he'd planned.

The people were pulling,
and the strings were snappin',
and the King was cursing,
and that's how it happened!

51

And when it was over,
a party broke out,
from the east to the west,
from the north to the south.

The King was crying,
he was all alone.
The Cranberry Clown
could hear him moan.

"Stop all your weeping!
There's nothing so tragic!
I've something to show you.
Come closer, it's magic!"

The King went down
to the clown by the cliff,
wiping his tears
with a handkerchief.

"What can YOU show me?"
the King only sighed.
"You're worse off than me!
At least I'm untied!"

"Everyone's tied,
it's not only me.
They're tied just the same,
with strings they can't see!"

"But isn't it sad
that you can't ride a bike?
Jump up and down,
or go for a hike?"

"Or swing on a swing,
or play the guitar,
or chase after ponies
no matter how far?"

"It's sad," said the clown,
"and sometimes I cry,
and sometimes I'm angry
and I shout at the sky!"

"Is somebody there?!!"
But nobody was.
"Will somebody help me?"
But nobody does.

"It's sad," said the clown,
"but it's beautiful, too,
when you know what I know,
and do what I do."

"What's that?" said the King,
with his eyes like an elf.
"Tell me, please, clown,
I must know for myself!"

"I close my eyes,
and I tip my chair,
and I hold my breath,
and I fall somewhere."

"And I fall so far,
and I fall so high,
that all I can say
is goodbye, goodbye."

"And faster and faster,
and farther I fall,
with nothing to catch me,
nothing at all!"

"And just when I fear
a fall never ceases,
I burst into colors,
I burst into pieces!"

"Pieces of where
and pieces of why,
pieces that drift
and fall from the sky."

"Pieces of laugh
and pieces of cry,
pieces of live
and pieces of die."

"And all I can say
is goodbye, goodbye!"

"But what does it mean?"
said the King, through his cloak.
"Does it mean that your life
is only a joke!"

"And what's left of you
after your fall?"
"Nothing," said the clown,
"nothing at all."

"Only the echoes
and shadows still live.
It's a small price to pay
for something to give!"

"Something to give?"
said the King in his greed.
"But mustn't you take
to get what you need?!!"

"Mustn't you clutch
and grasp with each fist?!!"
"How can I," said the clown,
"when I'm tied like this?"

"I can't make a move,
a false one or true.
I'm powerless," he said.
"Just like you!"

"It's a joke," said the clown,
"this life that we live,
when what we don't have
is what we must give."

"To burst into colors,
and pieces like stars,
and then echoes and shadows
is all that we are."

"It's a joke," said the clown,
"but it's not very clever,
for echoes and shadows
is all we were ever."

The King was smiling,
he finally knew,
knew what he wanted,
and what he must do.

He kissed the clown,
in a fond endeavor,
then he walked away,
and he was changed forever.

The clouds were white,
and the sky was gray,
the clown was quiet,
there was little to say.

He thought about freedom
and the damage it does,
he thought about magic
and how lucky he was.

He searched for reason
and he searched for rhyme,
and he searched the heavens
for one last time.

Then he closed his eyes,
and he tipped his chair,
and he held his breath
and he fell somewhere.

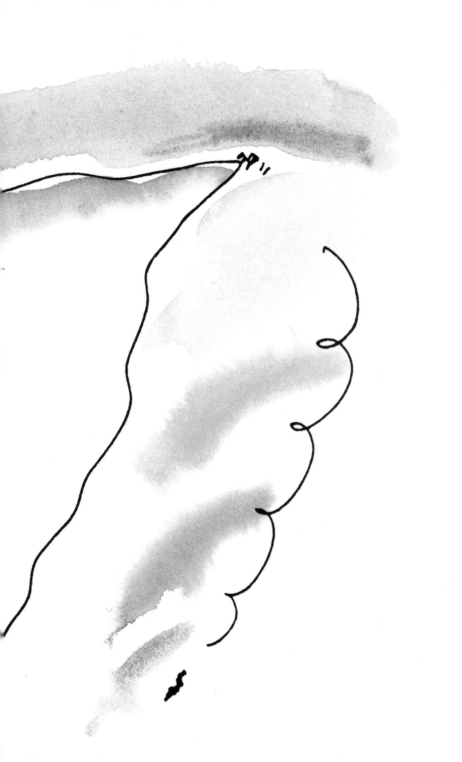

And he fell so far
and he fell so high
that all he could say
was "Goodbye, goodbye!"

So far and so high
so where and so why . . .

And all he could say
was "Goodbye, goodbye!"